# YOU CAN DRAW IT!

# SHARKS

WRITTEN BY MAGGIE ROSIER
ILLUSTRATED BY STEVE PORTER

BELLWETHER MEDIA · MINNEAPOLIS, MN

This edition first published in 2013 by Bellwether Media, Inc.

Library of Congress Cataloging-in-Publication Data
Rosier, Maggie.
    Sharks / by Maggie Rosier.
      pages cm. – (Express: you can draw it!)
    Includes bibliographical references and index.
    Summary: "Information accompanies step-by-step instructions on how to draw sharks. The text level and subject matter
are intended for students in grades 3 through 7"–Provided by publisher.
    ISBN 978-1-60014-901-6 (hardcover : alk. paper)
    1.  Sharks in art–Juvenile literature. 2.  Drawing–Technique–Juvenile literature.  I. Title.
    NC781.R67 2013
    743.6'73–dc23
                                   2012031543

Printed in the United States of America, North Mankato, MN.

# TABLE OF CONTENTS

# SHARKS!

A healthy fear of sharks is understandable. Some species, such as bull sharks and great whites, have attacked swimmers and surfers in coastal waters. Still, sharks are not the villains we make them out to be. These ocean marvels don't set out to sink their teeth into human flesh. They are, like many of us, fishers after a big catch.

DRAWING FROM PHOTOS IS A GREAT PLACE TO START. WORK YOUR WAY UP TO DRAWING FROM YOUR IMAGINATION.

*Before you begin drawing, you will need a few basic supplies.*

PAPER

DRAWING
PENCILS

## 2B OR NOT 2B?

NOT ALL DRAWING PENCILS ARE THE SAME. "B" PENCILS ARE SOFTER, MAKE DARKER MARKS, AND SMUDGE EASILY. "H" PENCILS ARE HARDER, MAKE LIGHTER MARKS, AND DON'T SMUDGE VERY MUCH AT ALL.

BLACK INK
PEN

COLORED PENCILS
(ALL DRAWINGS IN THIS BOOK WERE FINISHED WITH COLORED PENCILS.)

ERASER

PENCIL
SHARPENER

# Goblin Shark
## The Crazy-Faced Alien

The goblin shark is possibly the ugliest living shark. Its body is pink and flabby, and its snout looks like a beak. This underwater outcast stays in the dark depths of the ocean. When fish swim near, its jaws **protrude** with fang-like teeth to claim the meal!

## LIGHT TO DARK

BEGIN YOUR DRAWING WITH VERY LIGHT LINES. SLOWLY BUILD UP TO DARK LINES AS YOU REACH THE FINAL STEPS OF YOUR DRAWING. THIS WILL ALLOW FOR EASY CORRECTION OF MISTAKES.

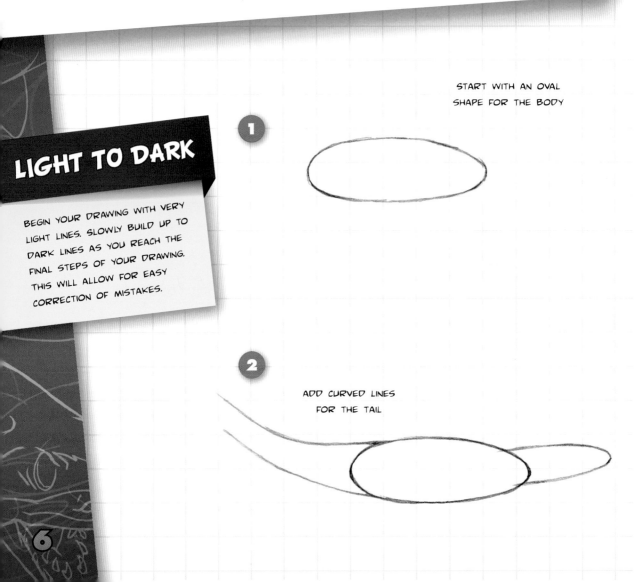

**1**

START WITH AN OVAL SHAPE FOR THE BODY

**2**

ADD CURVED LINES FOR THE TAIL

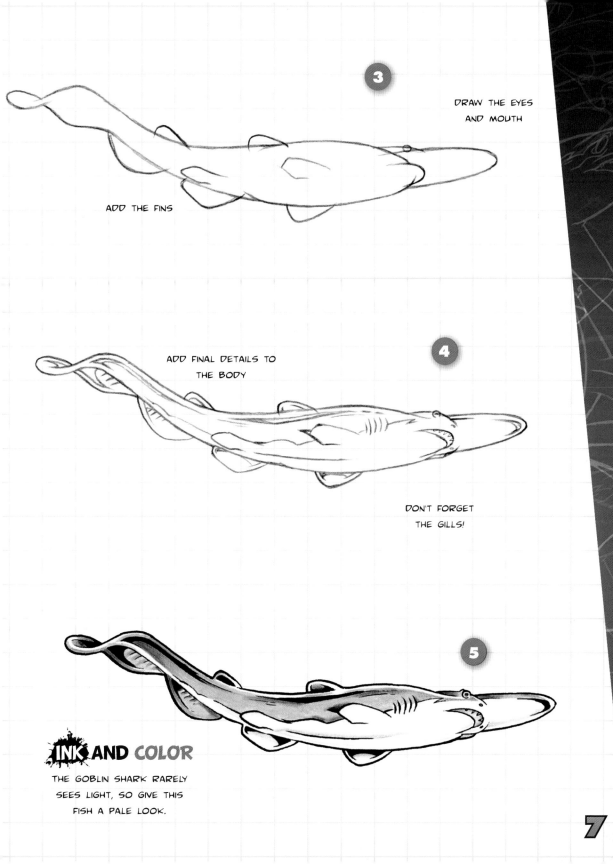

3

DRAW THE EYES
AND MOUTH

ADD THE FINS

ADD FINAL DETAILS TO
THE BODY

4

DON'T FORGET
THE GILLS!

5

INK AND COLOR

THE GOBLIN SHARK RARELY
SEES LIGHT, SO GIVE THIS
FISH A PALE LOOK.

7

# Great White Shark
## The Apex Predator

The great white shark offers underwater crowd control. This **apex predator** has complete authority over many ocean animals. As the largest predatory fish, the great white keeps prey populations in check. It often rockets out of the water to catch a seal. Sometimes it samples human flesh.

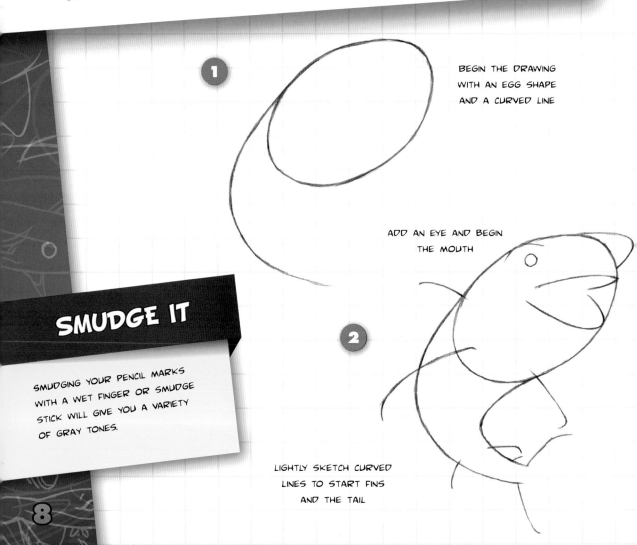

**1** BEGIN THE DRAWING WITH AN EGG SHAPE AND A CURVED LINE

ADD AN EYE AND BEGIN THE MOUTH

**2**

## SMUDGE IT

SMUDGING YOUR PENCIL MARKS WITH A WET FINGER OR SMUDGE STICK WILL GIVE YOU A VARIETY OF GRAY TONES.

LIGHTLY SKETCH CURVED LINES TO START FINS AND THE TAIL

**3**

ADD TEETH
AND GILLS

FINISH THE FINS
AND TAIL

ADD FINAL DETAILS
AND SHADING

**4**

**5**

## INK AND COLOR

LOOK OUT FOR THIS FIERCE
PREDATOR WITH A SLEEK, SILVER
BODY AND BRIGHT WHITE TEETH.

# Hammerhead Shark
## The Wide-Eyed Wonder

The hammerhead shark has a big head, but for good reason. It uses it to pin stingrays and other prey to the ocean floor. The size of its **cephalofoil** also gives the hammerhead a larger range of vision. This underwater hunter is tough to fool!

## USE YOUR ARM

DRAW WITH YOUR WHOLE ARM, NOT JUST YOUR WRIST AND FINGERS.

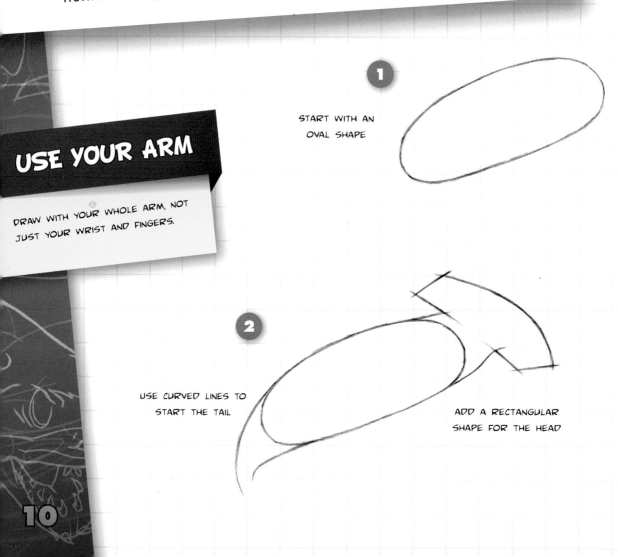

1

START WITH AN OVAL SHAPE

2

USE CURVED LINES TO START THE TAIL

ADD A RECTANGULAR SHAPE FOR THE HEAD

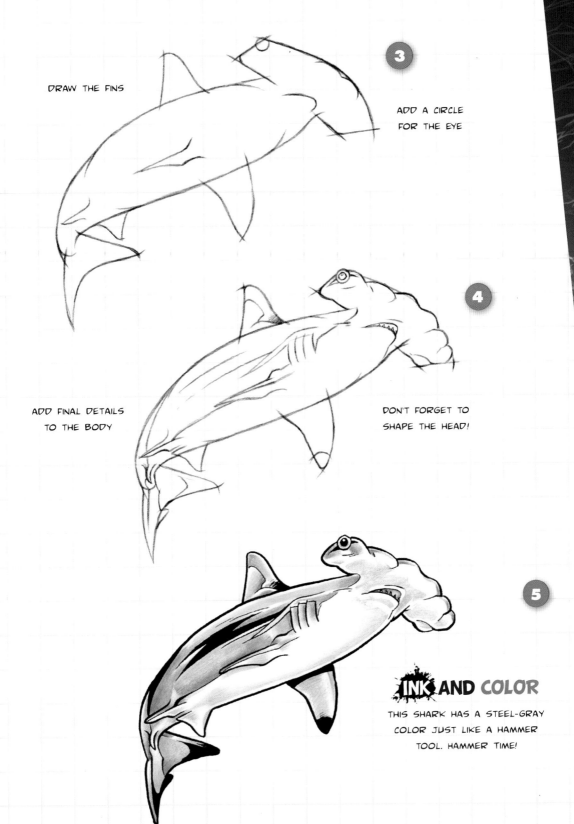

DRAW THE FINS

**3**

ADD A CIRCLE
FOR THE EYE

**4**

ADD FINAL DETAILS
TO THE BODY

DON'T FORGET TO
SHAPE THE HEAD!

**5**

INK AND COLOR

THIS SHARK HAS A STEEL-GRAY
COLOR JUST LIKE A HAMMER
TOOL. HAMMER TIME!

# Mako Shark
## The Leaping Speedster

Make way for the mako, the fastest shark in the sea! This slender fish has been clocked at more than 40 miles (64 kilometers) per hour. In addition to being fast, the mako has an impressive vertical. It can leap up to 20 feet (6 meters) above the surface of the water.

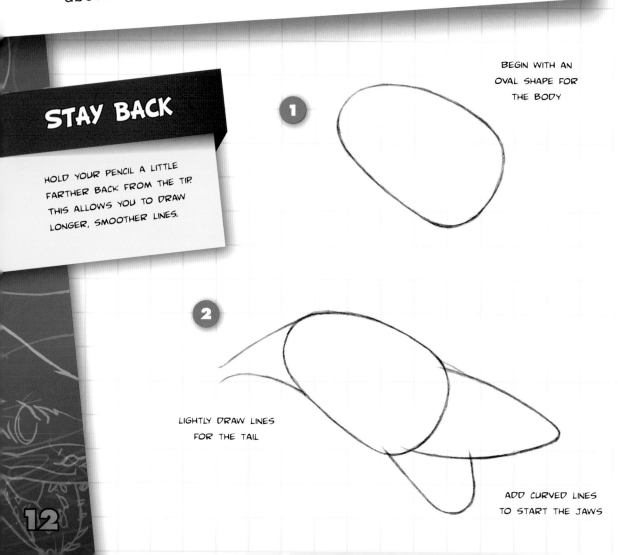

BEGIN WITH AN OVAL SHAPE FOR THE BODY

**1**

**2**

LIGHTLY DRAW LINES FOR THE TAIL

ADD CURVED LINES TO START THE JAWS

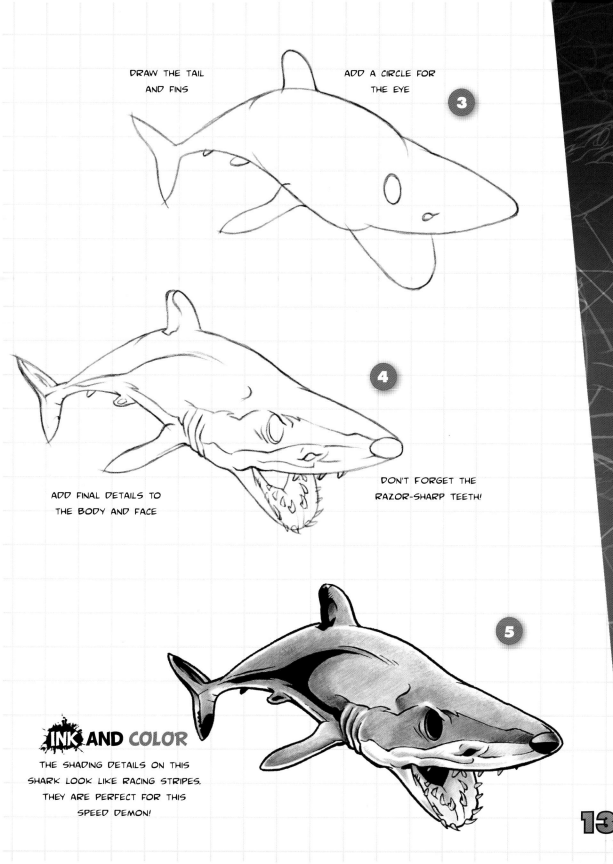

DRAW THE TAIL
AND FINS

ADD A CIRCLE FOR
THE EYE

3

4

ADD FINAL DETAILS TO
THE BODY AND FACE

DON'T FORGET THE
RAZOR-SHARP TEETH!

5

INK AND COLOR

THE SHADING DETAILS ON THIS
SHARK LOOK LIKE RACING STRIPES.
THEY ARE PERFECT FOR THIS
SPEED DEMON!

13

# Sand Tiger Shark
## The Toothy Terror

If any animal needs braces, it's the sand tiger shark. This fish has a mouthful of crooked teeth that make it look like more of a monster than it is. Smaller fish and other sea creatures should beware the sand tiger shark, but people have little to fear. This toothy terror is usually not aggressive toward humans.

## BREAK IT DOWN

JUST ABOUT ANY SUBJECT CAN BE BROKEN DOWN INTO SMALLER PARTS. LOOK FOR CIRCLES, OVALS, SQUARES, AND OTHER BASIC SHAPES THAT CAN HELP BUILD YOUR DRAWING.

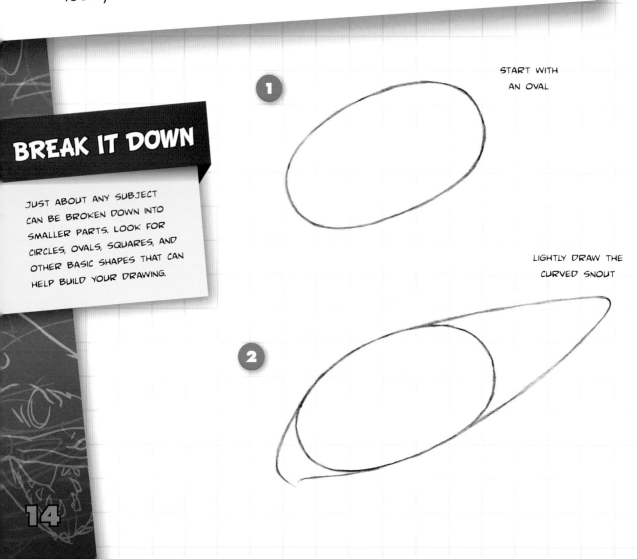

1

START WITH AN OVAL

2

LIGHTLY DRAW THE CURVED SNOUT

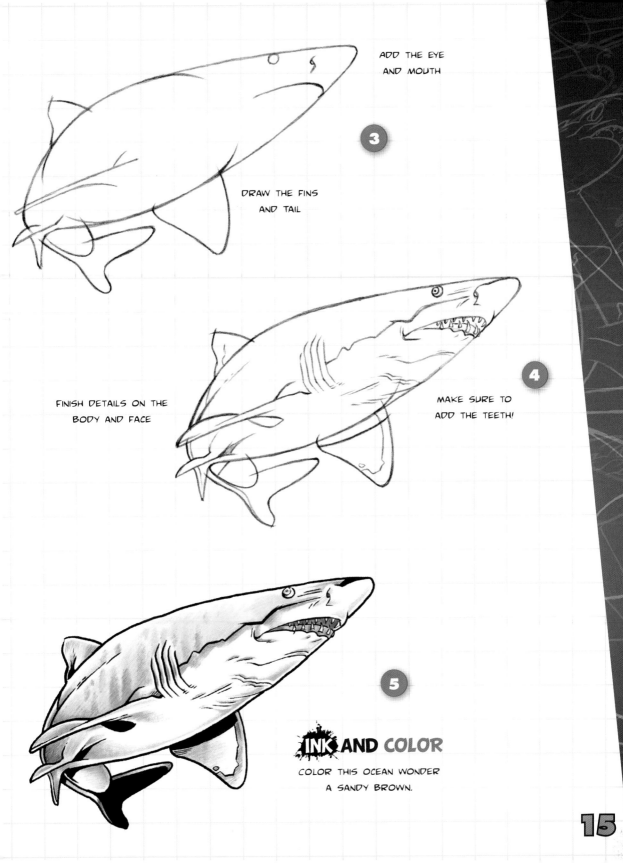

ADD THE EYE
AND MOUTH

3

DRAW THE FINS
AND TAIL

4

FINISH DETAILS ON THE
BODY AND FACE

MAKE SURE TO
ADD THE TEETH!

5

INK AND COLOR

COLOR THIS OCEAN WONDER
A SANDY BROWN.

15

# Saw Shark
## The Sharp-Nosed Slasher

The **slasher** of the sea, the saw shark cuts its victims with a blade-like snout. Sharp teeth **jut** out from the sides like the teeth of a saw. They alternate between long and short. The saw shark also sports a "mustache" of **barbels** that helps it locate prey.

START WITH AN
EGG SHAPE

**1**

## SEE THE BIG PICTURE

WAIT TO ADD DETAILS UNTIL YOU ARE HAPPY WITH THE BASIC SHAPE OF YOUR DRAWING. YOU DON'T WANT TO SPEND TIME DETAILING A PART OF YOUR DRAWING THAT WILL BE ERASED LATER.

OUTLINE THE SNOUT

**2**

DRAW FINS ON THE
TOP AND SIDES

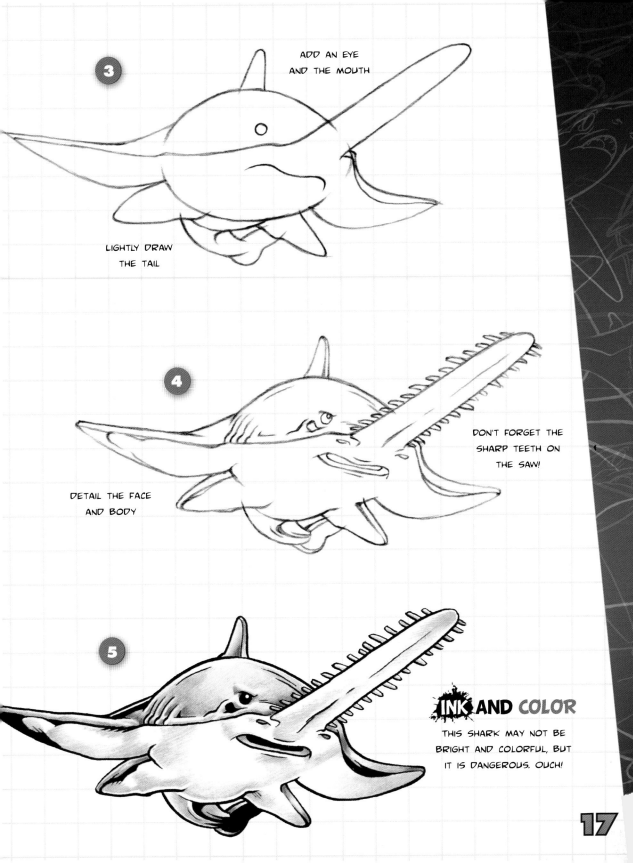

**3** ADD AN EYE AND THE MOUTH

LIGHTLY DRAW THE TAIL

**4** DETAIL THE FACE AND BODY

DON'T FORGET THE SHARP TEETH ON THE SAW!

**5**

**INK AND COLOR**

THIS SHARK MAY NOT BE BRIGHT AND COLORFUL, BUT IT IS DANGEROUS. OUCH!

# Thresher Shark
## The Tail Thrasher

The thresher shark **herds** before it hunts. It **thrashes** its large **caudal fin** to create whirlpools that trap smaller fish. Then it opens wide and takes its meal. The thresher shark's tail is its most valuable tool and one-third of its body weight!

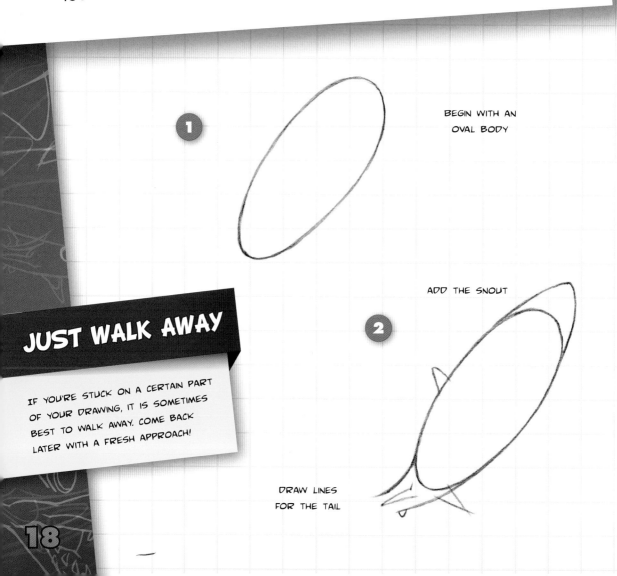

1 BEGIN WITH AN OVAL BODY

2 ADD THE SNOUT

DRAW LINES FOR THE TAIL

## JUST WALK AWAY

IF YOU'RE STUCK ON A CERTAIN PART OF YOUR DRAWING, IT IS SOMETIMES BEST TO WALK AWAY. COME BACK LATER WITH A FRESH APPROACH!

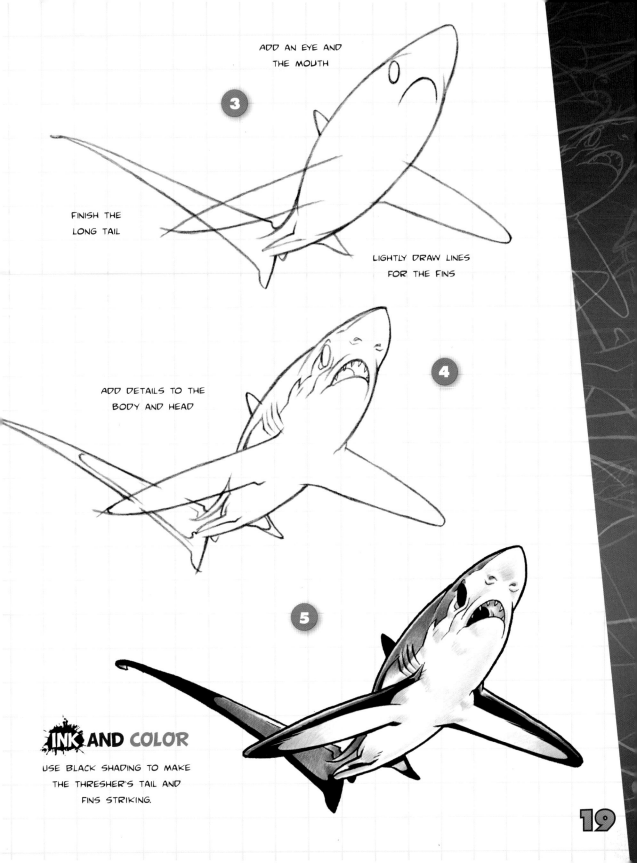

ADD AN EYE AND
THE MOUTH

**3**

FINISH THE
LONG TAIL

LIGHTLY DRAW LINES
FOR THE FINS

**4**

ADD DETAILS TO THE
BODY AND HEAD

**5**

# INK AND COLOR

USE BLACK SHADING TO MAKE
THE THRESHER'S TAIL AND
FINS STRIKING.

# Whale Shark
## The Spotted Giant

The whale shark opens its big mouth a lot! It is a **filter feeder**. When hungry, this shark sucks in water. The **plankton** and small fish unlucky enough to get pulled inside become dinner. Bigger fish and other ocean animals know the whale shark is not a threat. This spotted fish may be the largest in the sea, but it is a gentle giant.

## JUST A HINT

IT'S NOT NECESSARY TO INCLUDE EVERY SCALE AND SPOT ON YOUR SUBJECT. A FEW SCATTERED DETAILS CAN GIVE THE EFFECT. YOU CAN FINISH YOUR DRAWING A LITTLE FASTER THIS WAY.

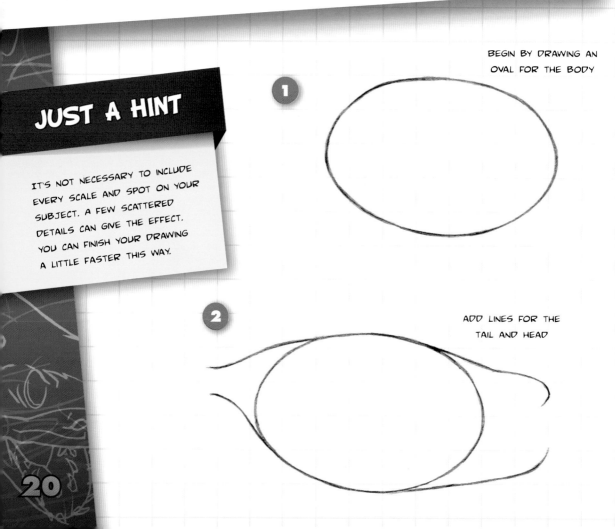

**1** BEGIN BY DRAWING AN OVAL FOR THE BODY

**2** ADD LINES FOR THE TAIL AND HEAD

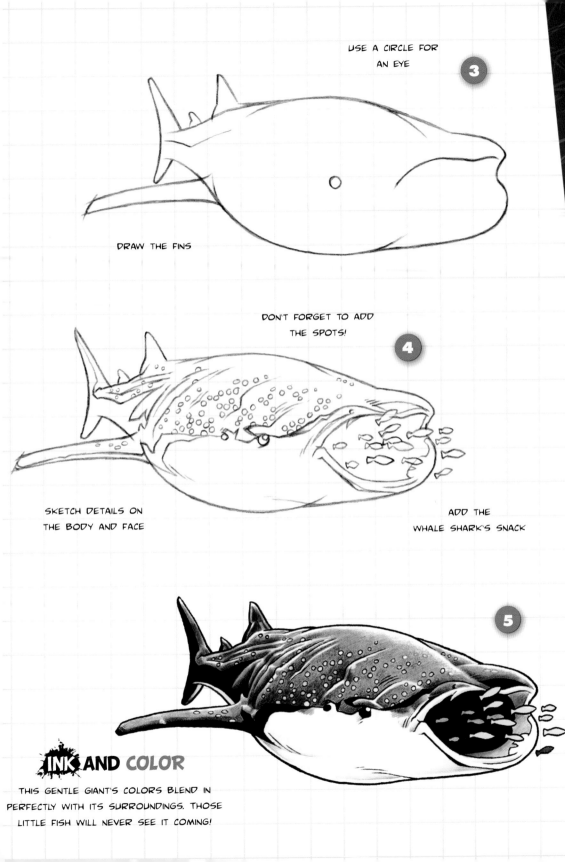

USE A CIRCLE FOR
AN EYE

**3**

DRAW THE FINS

DON'T FORGET TO ADD
THE SPOTS!

**4**

SKETCH DETAILS ON
THE BODY AND FACE

ADD THE
WHALE SHARK'S SNACK

**5**

# INK AND COLOR

THIS GENTLE GIANT'S COLORS BLEND IN
PERFECTLY WITH ITS SURROUNDINGS. THOSE
LITTLE FISH WILL NEVER SEE IT COMING!

# GLOSSARY

**apex predator**—a predator that is not hunted by any other animal

**barbels**—sensory organs that some fish have to help them locate food

**caudal fin**—the tail fin of a fish

**cephalofoil**—the wide, flat head of a hammerhead shark

**filter feeder**—an animal that eats by straining food particles and small fish from water

**herds**—gathers a group of animals together

**jut**—to extend outward or upward

**plankton**—tiny plants and animals that drift with ocean currents

**protrude**—to stick out

**slasher**—a person or animal that injures or kills with a sharp-edged blade

**thrashes**—moves about wildly and violently

## At the Library

Borgert-Spaniol, Megan. *The Whale Shark*. Minneapolis, Minn.: Bellwether Media, Inc., 2013.

Musgrave, Ruth. *National Geographic Kids Everything Sharks*. Washington, D.C.: National Geographic, 2011.

Van Briesen, Shawn. *Discovery Channel Top 10 Deadliest Sharks*. Horsham, Pa.: Zenescope Entertainment, 2010.

## On the Web

Learning more about sharks is as easy as 1, 2, 3.

1. Go to www.factsurfer.com.

2. Enter "sharks" into the search box.

3. Click the "Surf" button and you will see a list of related Web sites.

With factsurfer.com, finding more information is just a click away.

# INDEX